Private Law, Private Order

Justice and Security Without Government Interference

Rob Nielsen

Private Law, Private Order: Justice and Security Without Government Interference

ISBN 979-8-9957295-0-1 (Paperback Edition)

ISBN 979-8-9957295-1-8 (E-book Edition)

To the memory of Murray Rothbard, whose relentless pursuit of a stateless society and whose pioneering vision of private law and voluntary order continue to illuminate the path toward liberty on the centenary of his birth.

And to Hans-Hermann Hoppe, his foremost intellectual successor, who has defended and extended that vision with clarity and courage.

Table of Contents

Introduction

Imagine a world where justice isn't dispensed by distant bureaucrats or enforced through coercion and punishment, but emerges naturally from voluntary agreements, market competition, and mutual respect for rights. A world where security is designed to be like any other valuable service: innovative, customer-focused, and accountable, rather than a monopoly granted to the highest tax extractor. Most people dismiss this vision as utopian or dangerous, insisting that without government, society would descend into chaos. Yet history and reason tell a different story: private governance has repeatedly proven superior at protecting property, resolving disputes, and maintaining order, while government interference distorts justice, breeds inefficiency, and erodes morality.

We live in an era of unprecedented distrust in institutions. Polls show declining faith in governments worldwide, as overcriminalization, bloated prisons, endless wars, and corrupt enforcement reveal the state's true nature: not as a neutral protector, but as a coercive monopoly that expands at the expense of liberty. The fundamental question isn't whether we need law and order; it's who should provide it, and under what incentives. Government claims to be necessary, but its track record suggests otherwise, from the expansion of "criminal law" to replace restitution-based systems, to perverse incentives that reward punishment over prevention. As Gustave de Molinari observed over a century ago, a state monopoly on security leads to the very abuses it purports to prevent.

This book challenges that monopoly head-on. Drawing from thinkers like Lysander Spooner, who distinguished true crimes (harm to others) from mere vices, and Thomas Paine, who recognized that much of society's order stems from mutual dependence rather than authoritarian government, we explore how private, consensual mechanisms can deliver genuine justice and security. At the heart of the argument are Security Assurance Organizations (SAOs)—private agencies bundling protection, insurance, arbitration, and enforcement. These entities would compete to offer the best value: screening members for risk, incentivizing good behavior through lower premiums, preventing conflicts ex ante with technology and deterrence, and resolving disputes ex post through restitution, arbitration, and reputation-based ostracism.

Unlike state systems, private order aligns incentives with outcomes. Victims receive direct compensation rather than seeing fines funneled into government coffers. Agencies invest in prevention because payouts hurt their bottom line. Reputation and freedom of association create powerful deterrents that are far more effective than prisons that often breed more crime. Historical precedents abound: Anglo-Saxon tythings for mutual pledges, medieval competing courts that improved efficiency through rivalry (as Adam Smith noted), and the Law Merchant's voluntary customary rules. Even today, private arbitration dominates commercial disputes, and emerging technologies like blockchain and smart contracts lower barriers to decentralized enforcement.

Government, in contrast, suffers systemic failures: moral contradictions (violating natural rights through taxation and conscription), lack of knowledge (unable to calculate optimal justice), incentive problems (perverse rewards for overreach), and lack of accountability (immunity from consequences). The minarchist hope that a minimal state can be contained collapses under the same dynamics that cause all monopolies to grow. As

Spooner concluded about the Constitution, it has either authorized the abusive government we have or has proven powerless to prevent it. In either case, it is unfit.

This is not mere theory. Declining trust in the state, combined with technological tools that enable voluntary coordination, points toward a practical transition. Private solutions aren't perfect. They require peaceful people, strong morality, and cultural support. But they outperform coercion every time they are allowed to compete.

In the pages ahead, we examine the private foundations of social order, the mechanics of private law (from ex ante prevention to ex post restitution), the hierarchy of consequences (culminating in disassociation), and why government interference perverts what private systems achieve naturally. We compare the two paradigms side-by-side and conclude with optimism: liberty advances not through revolution, but through education, innovation, and the quiet withdrawal of consent from failing institutions.

If you've ever questioned why the state claims a monopoly on force yet delivers so little true security, or if you're ready to envision a more free and just society, this book is for you. Let's explore what law and order look like when built on consent, not coercion.

Choice and Governance

People are not all the same, and they make different choices because they have different values, circumstances, and levels of understanding. Sometimes those choices are peaceful and wise; sometimes they are not. So what are the best ways to promote good choices and cooperation while preventing and providing resolution for conflict?

In answering such questions, it is important to recognize that there are unavoidable limitations. The idea of a perfect society where there is no conflict and all outcomes are equal is an absurd utopian fantasy, and so is the idea of a deus ex machina that can magically swoop in to make everything right. Imperfect knowledge and ability, conflicting interests, transaction costs, and other collective action problems will always be barriers to a perfectly peaceful and productive society.

In economic terms, there are markets for law and order just like there are markets for food and clothing. They are composed of scarce goods whose supply is in demand and which must be allocated among competing uses. Economic analysis of governance mechanisms offers tremendous insights, not least of all because it accounts for the crucial impact of incentives and constraints on human behavior.

History and reason show that private governance does an excellent job of protecting property rights and facilitating peaceful exchange. They also show that government interference distorts and obstructs justice.

Principles of Justice

Justice is the preservation and restoration of rights under natural law, and is required for peace and harmony in society. Justice is also the foundation upon which mercy and charity must be built. Victims may choose to grant mercy to violators to appease the demands of justice, but denying justice to victims leads to perpetual conflict and misery.

True justice is based on protection and restitution, not revenge. Two wrongs can't make a right. Retaliation tends to escalate conflict and waste resources, often at the expense of victims. Restitution compensates victims, eliminates desires for revenge, and provides contrite offenders with a path to redemption.

Violations of natural law are always violations of property rights. This is obvious with typical property crimes like theft, but even your life and liberty are based on self-ownership. This underscores the importance of clear property rights because without them, there is no basis for victimhood or restitution. No property, no victim. No victim, no violation.

Rights violations in a free society would be treated as torts. Many offenses currently considered "crimes" would still be illegal, but compulsory puritanism would be unlikely. Proponents of victimless crime laws (e.g. laws against drug use or prostitution) are rarely willing to bear the costs of enforcing them.

> Vices are those acts by which a man harms himself or his property. Crimes are those acts by which one man harms the person or property of another. Vices are simply the errors which a man makes in his search after his own happiness. Unlike crimes, they imply no malice toward others, and no interference with their persons or property.
> LYSANDER SPOONER

Law and Order in a Free Society

The Private Underpinnings of Social Order

> Great part of that order which reigns among mankind is not the effect of government. It has its origin in the principles of society and the natural constitution of man. It existed prior to government, and would exist if the formality of government was abolished. The mutual dependence and reciprocal interest which man has upon man, and all the parts of civilised community upon each other, create that great chain of connection which holds it together.
> THOMAS PAINE

Social order is not a simple question of getting the right words on paper and people with weapons threatening to enforce them. If that were so, then dropping constitutions and guns on people would result in civilization and prisons would be the safest places on earth.

A society cannot rise above the beliefs, abilities, and behaviors of individuals and families. Individuals are the foundational unit of families, and family is the foundational unit of society. If your goal is a peaceful, productive society, then you need peaceful, productive people. Peaceful, productive people tend to come from and promote functional, intact families. If the majority of people in a group are ignorant, violent orphans, no system of laws can effectively address such a problem and arming uniformed guards (who would also be largely ignorant, violent orphans) would only make addressing it more difficult.

The impact of morality and good families on civilization is irreplaceable. A culture that promotes and incentivizes moral behavior and nuclear family structure does more to advance civilization than any kind of large-scale enforcement of dictated law possibly could. Some forms of external governance will always be necessary, but the more people govern themselves, the fewer resources need to be devoted to external governance.

Freedom of Association

> The fundamental principle for describing a free society is the principle of freedom of association. A first corollary of this principle is the freedom of disassociation.
> CHANDRAN KUKATHAS

When people are free to choose whom they associate with, they tend to self-select into groups of people who have similar values and reputations. Civilized people tend to choose to trade with each other, help each other, and create voluntary associations to facilitate peaceful exchange and promote good behavior. They also tend to choose not to associate with people who are not civilized. This means that violent, lazy, degenerate people are often excluded from civilized people in a free society until and unless they choose to become peaceful, productive, and civilized.

The natural inclination to self-select into (or out of) communities with different rules and characteristics is fundamental. When freedom of association is denied, it causes conflict and undermines voluntary associations that depend on and encourage self-governance, resulting in civilizational decline.

The Private Origins of Common Law

> The landholder, the farmer, the manufacturer, the merchant, the tradesman, and every occupation, prospers by the aid which each receives from the other, and from the whole. Common interest regulates their concerns, and forms their law; and the laws which common usage ordains, have a greater influence than the laws of government. In fine, society performs for itself almost everything which is ascribed to government.
> THOMAS PAINE

Markets precede governments, and that includes markets for governance mechanisms. Customary law is based on cooperation induced by reciprocities. Such cooperation clearly does not require government action, since it has always preceded government. Reciprocity also provides the basis for recognition of obligation under such laws. Many people believe that modern legal systems are a result of benevolent government monopoly, but the development of Anglo-American common law actually has private origins.

Before the Norman invasion of 1066 in England, free men banded together to form groups called tythings that met together for mutual benefit and pledged to honor judgments against their members within and between tything groups. Individuals found guilty of wrongdoing in a trial who chose to ignore a judgment were ostracized from the group and lost the privileges of participation in that system.

In medieval and early modern England, various kinds of courts competed for cases. Some of the courts were general and based on geography or membership, such as local, hundred, manorial, county, chancery, and common-law courts. Some were specialized like merchant courts and ecclesiastical courts. Even when royal courts and the King's Bench came along and claimed official jurisdiction, parties in dispute could choose a different court to hear the case.

As a result of competition in the market for legal services, those services became more efficient and more fair. Adam Smith wrote in The Wealth of Nations that "During the improvement of the law of England there arose rivalships among the several courts," and said that due to competition, "each court endeavoured, by superior dispatch and impartiality, to draw to itself as many causes as it could." Just as in other markets, the rules and regulations of the market for law came endogenously from the market itself. Smith also said that "[a]nother thing which tended to support the liberty of the people and render the proceedings in the courts very exact, was the rivalship which arose betwixt them."

Private Governance

The demands for order and security in society are very strong, and providers of private governance meet those demands. What does private governance look like?

Private governance mechanisms are all around you. They are in the clubs you join and the insurance you buy. They are in sports leagues and churches. They are in your credit score and automated home security systems. They are in blockchain technology and personal security smart phone applications. They are in internet market platform merchant policies, payment processors, package tracking, money-back guarantees, and digital encryption. They are in arbitration clauses in employment contracts and private divorce mediation and dispute resolution.

They are in self-defense classes, neighborhood watch groups, night watchmen, security guards, and bodyguards. They are in escrow services, in the bylaws of stock markets, and the terms of the most complex financial transactions in the world. They are in credit cards and personal loans. They are in industry watchdog groups and professional certification associations. They are in security deposits, the bonding agency of your plumber, and the ethical standards of private schools. These are only examples of common and effective private governance mechanisms, and it is impossible to predict what kinds of solutions innovative entrepreneurs will develop in the future.

Private governance mechanisms are necessary and exist in all societies to varying degrees, and they perform better the more free they are from government interference. In a free society, a larger variety of individual and cooperative security arrangements would be available. Some people may choose to take the responsibilities of providing security for themselves in their own hands. Perhaps they have a high tolerance for risk, or maybe they live in conditions where the risk to their life and property are very low.

However, most people choose to cooperate with each other to mitigate such risks or transfer them to third parties, especially when the cost to do so is relatively low. For example, people choose to transfer assets and risks to financial institutions and insurance companies because they prefer to trust organizations designed to protect assets and make them available upon request or in response to a risk event, especially if that organization agrees to a return on those funds in exchange for specific limitations and terms of use.

Market forces of supply and demand will determine the variety and evolution of the security industry, but there are very good reasons to expect insurance-like arrangements would continue to grow. Bundled solutions that provide for monitoring, protection, investigation, compensation, dispute resolution, and enforcement would be especially compelling.

Private firms that specialize in personal security, property protection, and dispute resolution would operate much like mutual insurance agencies. We could call them Security Assurance Organizations or SAOs for short. SAOs would offer various solutions, likely with discounts for bundling them together. They would provide protection for their customers, insure them against loss, represent them in formal disputes, and provide for enforcement as necessary.

The level of service you could expect from such agencies would be much higher than you may think. Why? I can see several reasons:

- They have strong incentives to please their customers. If they fail to attract or satisfy customers, they will fail very rapidly. The prospect of profit is a market signal of revocable consent.
- They have strong incentives to innovate due to competition with other agencies. Just look at how cell phone technologies and networks evolve.
- They have strong incentives to demonstrate credibility and transparent alignment to reciprocal industry standards. Competition and reciprocity aren't just incentives for innovation; they are also incorruptible regulators.
- They have strong incentives to prevent security violations, as it would yield a greater profit than using additional resources to respond to them.

- Some would become highly specialized to take advantage of the benefits of division of labor in the service of customers with unique needs.
- They would integrate vertically and horizontally to take advantage of value chain optimization and economies of scale.
- They would cooperate with each other for the mutual benefit of the network effect based on standard rules and reciprocal agreements, much like cell phone companies and insurance companies do now.
- They would offer customized solutions for those with varying budgets, preferences, reputations, circumstances, geographical areas, etc. Why buy more or less than you want or need?
- They would not be artificially limited by political boundaries.
- They could incentivize communities and travel agencies to meet safety standards, allowing them to offer special assurances and discounts, as well as reduce their overhead and pass on savings to members who live and travel in standards-compliant circumstances.
- They would not be considered above the law. Without a geographical monopoly on adjudication and enforcement, they would be unable to rely on willing and/or helpless victims. If they were to misbehave, their customers, competitors, and industry partners would quickly publicize their bad behavior, hold them accountable/liable, and even boycott or ostracize them if necessary.
- They would have a bias for peaceful resolution. Conflict is very expensive (in terms of both resources and risk of additional harm), and when you are spending your own

money, you have strong incentives to choose and innovate solutions that deal with conflict in the most rapid and peaceful ways possible. Even when direct physical intervention could be justified in some cases does not mean that other options would not be preferable.

The conflict-averse incentives and preferences of SAOs would also naturally extend to their members and customers. Potential members would be screened for previous provocative behavior like escalating conflict or vigilantism, as such behavior would increase risk (and the financial, legal, and reputational costs associated with that risk).

Rules Without Rulers

Private associations have their own rules to incentivize good behavior of members and exclude those who do not want to agree to them. But what rules would there be between different organizations or those who choose not to participate in them?

In the case of formal contractual agreements, terms often include self-enforcing ex ante mechanisms like escrow, bonds, reputation mechanisms, and pricing risk into terms like interest rates. They also frequently make use of what is known as compromissum, which is an agreement to abide by arbitration conditions stipulated in the contract itself should there be a dispute.

With private property rights and reciprocity (i.e. self-evident natural law) already established as the origin and basis for common law, private parties and arbitrators would continue to cooperate in discovering, optimizing, and customizing the application of rules and procedures. Under such a decentralized but integrated system of conflict avoidance and peacekeeping, the discipline of constant dealings between SAOs and arbitration agencies would promote handling disagreements by provisions and procedures agreed upon by everyone in advance. The rules that best serve the reciprocal interests of parties in dispute would be freely adopted as agency policy and perhaps even industry standard practice, while those that do not would be abandoned. As previously mentioned, anyone refusing to resolve disputes in a peaceful manner (whether they participate in an SAO or not) would be subject to exclusion and the resulting loss of benefits related to being a member of polite society.

Not only would such a decentralized model tend toward adopting the most beneficial rules, it would also tend toward adopting the right amount of rules for given situations. In the same way that price discovery in a free market leads to an equilibrium between supply and demand of goods and services, rule discovery in a free market also tends toward an equilibrium between the costs and benefits of rules. In economic terms, the marginal, gross, and net benefits and costs of rules would continually be optimized, since providers of private governance have incentives to constantly discover and adopt the best ways of preventing and solving problems.

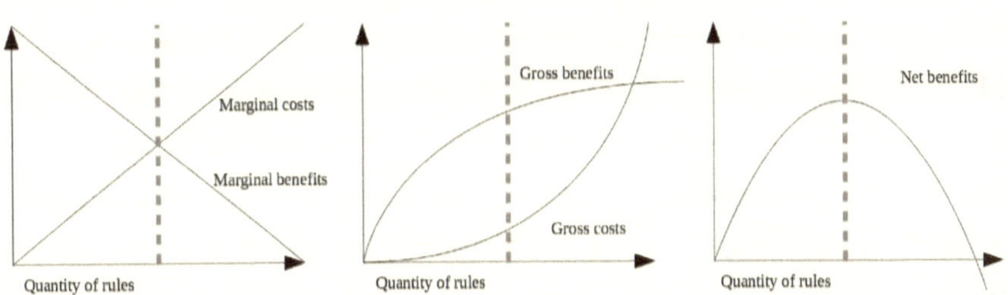

Figure 1: The dotted lines in the image above represent the optimal number of rules based on costs and benefits. Only rules whose benefits exceed costs should be adopted. Some rules are good, but too many rules can detract from the benefits and eventually make participants worse off than if there were no rules at all.

Ex Ante Solutions

> An ounce of prevention is worth a pound of cure. BENJAMIN FRANKLIN, founder of the oldest property insurance organization in the United States.

Many private governance mechanisms are designed to address issues ex ante (before the event) rather than ex post (after the event) because it is more cost effective, safe, and efficient to do so.

In a market free of government interference, security issues are risk management problems and business opportunities. Individuals and SAOs would have strong incentives to avoid problems first, cooperate rapidly to resolve disputes second, and only physically restrain and remove predators as a last resort. The earlier in that process they can employ effective solutions, the more safety and prosperity they can enjoy.

Private associations can set membership requirements and screen members for good behavior. The simple ability to screen or exclude unwanted members gives such clubs a powerful tool to discourage bad behavior without relying on the use of force. Membership requirements and screening processes enable people to self-select into associations where members are interested in following a common set of rules. Membership requirements and policy pricing related to risk assessment also provide incentives for people to behave. For example, SAOs could offer lower premiums to those with long, peaceful track records, and those with a history of bad behavior would pay higher premiums and perhaps be required to submit to increased monitoring or other requirements to become or remain a member.

While free markets provide customers with deterrent tools like fences, locks, cameras, lighting, etc., SAO members would likely either be provided with them as a benefit of being a member/policyholder, or incentivized to employ and update them with discounted premium rates for doing so. It is also worth noting that while it deserves a separate discussion, private gun ownership is a major deterrent on crime of all kinds. It is no coincidence that private gun ownership and violent crime are inversely correlated.

SAOs would make use of market solutions for trust problems in order to attract and retain members. Services for due diligence, trusted associate networks and approved intermediaries (with money-back guarantees), contracts, escrow, physical deposits, and letters of credit would make sophisticated arrangements and transactions more safe, reliable, and efficient. Advances in technology standards like encryption and blockchain continue to provide even more assurances of security and privacy.

SAOs would also contract with threat management organizations to perform various watchfulness, education/training, and conflict avoidance functions. There are more private security guards than government law enforcement personnel in the United States, Britain, and Canada, despite the forced funding and increasing militarization of "public" police.

Ex Post Solutions

In responding to a security incident, the primary objective of an SAO would be de-escalation of conflict in the interest of protecting people and property. Escalation of a conflict would increase the risk of a violent outcome and the loss of resources and reputation that would accompany it. In very rare cases, violence may be required to stop direct threats. In such cases, private agencies are very careful to adhere to justifiable guidelines in order to protect themselves and their clients.

Once an offense has occurred, an SAO is obligated to determine whether there is a valid claim to be made against an offender. If so, the SAO would first compensate the victim. With the victim made whole, the SAO would then seek restitution from the offender. If the offender were represented by an SAO, the two organizations would promptly settle the claim through negotiation/mediation/arbitration and make restitution as necessary. If the two parties cannot easily establish the validity of the claim, they would use a private adjudicator to provide a judgment. By virtue of compromissum and the discipline of constant dealings, all parties involved consent to the process and are obligated to abide by the results. If the accused were found guilty, his SAO would compensate the prosecuting SAO for restitution as well as any costs associated with investigation and resolution. If the accused were not found guilty, his SAO would be entitled to compensation for adjudication and related costs. In either case, victims with legitimate claims are compensated right away and the responsibility for collecting restitution from offenders lies with their own chosen agencies.

Of course, individuals may choose to represent themselves in such matters rather than rely on the services of an SAO or other agencies. They would also be free to change their mind and seek assistance with legal matters on whatever terms they choose.

If this kind of private arbitration seems unlikely, you should consider that the great majority of large corporations already have arbitration clauses in their consumer contracts and almost all do in their employment contracts. You have almost surely signed private arbitration agreements with your credit card company, cell phone carrier, and more. Private adjudication has been around for many hundreds of years and is thriving in our complex modern world for resolving disputes large and small, government claims of jurisdiction notwithstanding.

Private Legal Processes and Procedures

The vast majority of disputes can be avoided or resolved without private adjudication. It is not a panacea for every potential dispute, but private parties have incentives to arrange for it when it can benefit them.

The processes and procedures of private adjudication are often bundled as pre-dispute clauses with the compromissum of a contract. This internalizes the costs and benefits to the contracting parties, maximizes joint benefit, and minimizes potential bias or waste.

Rather than impose a single solution on all cases, parties in dispute can choose the processes and procedures that best fit their situation. What is the right balance to strike between tradeoffs like speed/accuracy, formal/informal, standard/custom, expedited/thorough, confidential/transparent, and adversarial/collaborative? The parties in dispute (to whom costs and benefits have been largely internalized) have the proper incentives to choose the optimal solution. Consider for example the solutions that JAMS Alternative Dispute Resolution offers to parties in dispute from what it calls the alternative dispute resolution spectrum:

<u>Direct Negotiation</u>
Court-appointed special masters / discovery masters
Neutral expert fact-finding
Nonbinding arbitration
Minitrial
Neutral evaluation
Evaluative mediation
Facilitative mediation
Mediative processes

<u>Adjudicative Processes</u>
Med-Arb (mediation with optional appeal to arbitration)
Private Judging
Final-offer arbitration
Bracketed arbitration
Arbitration

Features like pretrial discovery and multiple levels of appeals can be beneficial, but they can also be extremely costly. Interestingly, most disputing private parties opt out of such features, preferring low costs, swift resolutions, and minimized escalation.

Where appeals are desirable, dispute resolution arrangements could specify an appeals procedure, including a limit on the number of appeals. Given that there are two parties to a dispute, a decision arrived at by any two courts would be a reasonable way to confirm a decision. That would allow potential disagreements by the preferred court of each disputant to be settled by a pre-selected appeals court. There would be no one "supreme" court, but government systems do not guarantee that appeals will be reviewed by supreme courts, anyway.

Other features such as trial by jury would be supplied if desired, but they would be relatively more expensive, and would thus be less likely. But that also makes sense given that jury trials became desirable in the first place largely because they offered some protection from hostile judges imposed by government courts. When the parties in dispute choose their own judges, such protections are less relevant.

Judges under such a system would be incentivized to produce the most clear, consistent, and impartial opinions possible, as it would be the basis for their reputation and business. Such opinions would have influence on industry best practices and policies due to their ability to minimize the number of disputes that require adjudication and provide consistent guidance as precedent for those that do.

As for policies of the courts themselves, experience has shown that in order to satisfactorily end disputes and enjoy the verification of their decisions by those in dispute as well as other interested parties, private courts must openly publicize their procedures in detail, allow transparent third-party observation of proceedings (with certain exceptions for some privacy and related concerns), and make accurate records of proceedings available.

While it is possible that some SAOs could isolate themselves by refusing to arrange for smooth conflict resolution with other communities and agencies, there are reasons why it is very unlikely. First, conflict avoidance and resolution is their entire reason for existing. If they can't find ways to avoid conflict (especially with other conflict avoiding entities), they will not be in business long. Second, there are substantial economies of standardization in reciprocal working relationships with other agencies. Third, the discipline of constant dealings would naturally produce arrangements between agencies (not unlike treaties) for things like arrest and extradition where necessary (not to mention the previously discussed multi-lateral reputation tracking). In essence, agencies provide both checks and balances for each other as well as economies of scale and standardization. Such "co-opetition" mutually benefits all parties.

If a community felt very strongly that they wanted to impose laws that are outside typical standards (probably religious in origin), they would have strong incentives to make those rules clear and arrange for consistent treatment of outsiders so as to avoid consequences that result in economic isolation and property devaluation. In a free society, no community can long enforce its will on outsiders without the support of outsiders. That being said, history has shown that good laws are spread and adopted quickly between jurisdictions because they are efficient at preventing and avoiding conflict. For example, see the development of the Lex Mercatoria in Western Europe.

Effective Consequences and Efficient Enforcement

Fines are the most convenient way to compensate victims for their losses. Other terms could certainly be worked out between parties in dispute, especially before resorting to formal adjudication. However, fines also have several other important advantages as the default form of restitution.

Advantages of fines as restitution:

- Fines can be planned for and secured by voluntary agreement, just like other contract and insurance arrangements.
- Guaranteed payment for fines can be issued to victims without unnecessary delay.
- The right to collect a fine (like other property rights) is transferable, along with the risk and expense of pursuing offenders and recovering the payment. This provides a natural incentive for powerful groups to prosecute those who harm the poor and weak. It also shields victims from unnecessarily spending additional time and energy on negative experiences. It also doesn't require a victim to have a prior arrangement with an SAO, since they could sell the right to collect restitution to an agency after an offense has occurred, if they choose.
- Fines could incentivize rapid resolution of disputes, by requiring bonds that cover damages and enforcement costs to be posted prior to escalating a dispute to expensive adjudication.
- The responsibility to pay fines and post bail bonds can also be transferred to a third party. An accused offender's SAO or community (whether geographic or functional) could pay or extend credit for restitution to the victim as a bond and hold the offender accountable for it on their end. This also protects victims from the results of accused offenders who flee from resolution.
- Fines for restitution actually compensate victims, reducing anger and making subsequent violence, revenge, and feuds

less likely. Offenders also get the opportunity to bring back the peace and claim their place in civilized society.

Calculating fines could be done in various ways, but is likely to resemble something like this simple and reasonable formula:

(Damages + Enforcement Costs) / Probability of Successful Prosecution

For example, let's say a car was stolen. If the car is worth $10,000 and approximately one third of car thefts are successfully solved, the only question left is enforcement costs. If the offender is identified and confesses, the cost will be lower. If the accused is guilty, but still wants to argue about it, their liability will go up significantly. Resulting in something like this:

($10,000 + Enforcement Costs) / .33

The fine in this case would be at least $30,000, which is approximately triple the damages (much more if they insist on dragging out the dispute to cover the costs of enforcement). All this for a car that a thief could perhaps sell in a hurry to a shady dealer at a likely price of less than $5,000. When the risk to a car thief is at least six times greater than the expected benefit, there are strong rational incentives not to steal cars. There are also strong incentives for guilty parties to settle disputes quickly to avoid increasing their liability, which also extends to any agency representing them.

Restitution of costs is naturally owed to those who are acquitted of an offense as well (since they are victims of false accusation), including any investigation on their behalf. This especially benefits the poor and disadvantaged who otherwise could not afford to have agencies with equal power to those of an

accuser work on their behalf. This simple principle is a powerful
deterrent against frivolous lawsuits and trolls, and makes
deliberate or accidental conviction of the innocent far less
feasible. It is also a very powerful deterrent against abuse by
security officers, who would be subject to fines for falsifying
violations, falsely charging innocent people of wrongdoing, or
bullying (not to mention likely to be fired from their jobs by
employers who need to protect their reputation and avoid the
liabilities and risks associated with dishonest and abusive
employees).

Disassociation and Ostracism

Like private ex ante solutions, private ex post solutions are
based in freedom of association and disassociation, resulting in
foundational strategies of exclusion, boycott, and ostracism.
Credible threats of ostracism are non-invasive, but can be very
effective at incentivizing good behavior.

Consider how in the sport of basketball a player who
commits five fouls is ejected from the game. Most players (even
aggressive ones) avoid committing five fouls because they do not
want to be excluded from the benefits of playing the game (in
addition to the negative consequences associated with each
infraction). The exclusion of players who do not comply with the
rules (not to mention the negative treatment from one's own
teammates and coaches) is enough to incentivize compliance with
the rules. If a player were to fight against ejection from a single
game, his entire career would be at risk.

When one's reputation and trustworthiness are tracked and
the ability to participate in organized society can become very
expensive or even be lost entirely, all but the most foolish,
desperate, and recalcitrant will play by the rules. The cost in terms

of potential employers, lenders, travel agencies, protection services, customers and many others refusing to work with people who have a reputation for rejecting fair play makes complying with even questionable judgments preferable to the alternative. This is even more true when you consider the potential influence of location- and jurisdiction-independent technology-enhanced multi-lateral reputation-tracking mechanisms on modern life.

One vivid historical example of disassociation in action is the origin of the word "boycott" itself. In 1880, locals in County Mayo, Ireland organized against Charles Boycott, who was a land agent enforcing high rents and evictions during difficult times. Rather than resort to violence or appeal to state courts, the community, guided by the Irish Land League, simply withdrew all cooperation: workers quit, shops refused service, neighbors shunned him. The campaign was so effective that Boycott was isolated and eventually left Ireland. Newspapers worldwide adopted his last name as a verb to describe organized refusal of dealings as a form of protest or enforcement.

What does effective ostracism in modern society look like? It is being unable to borrow money (due to credit reporting) or buy and sell property (due to liens and title restrictions) or rent an apartment (landlord background check service) or having your employment terminated (dependent on employment contract) or not being able to travel easily (through agency compliance with accreditation requirements) or being unable to contract for protection services (due to unaffordable risk), or being exposed as dishonest and dangerous to significant others (background check for verified dating sites/services). These and other mechanisms can scale together to form quite a formidable combination of peaceful, consensual non-association systems.

Of course, ostracism need not be permanent. When people tire of being excluded from civilized society, they can redeem themselves by arranging for clearance of their debts and establishing a good reputation. Debt settlement and credit repair services already serve a similar function.

Even large organizations are kept in check through threat of ostracism. Throughout history, international commercial law has been enforced through threat of boycott by other merchants for violating contract, for example. The benefits of cooperation and reciprocity are just too great to walk away from, even (perhaps especially) for those with great wealth and influence.

Imprisonment Alternatives and Rehabilitation

Prisons create a lot of problems. Not only do they fail to compensate victims, they put the burdens of prison construction, maintenance, and operation on the victims as well. Prisons are also counterproductive. They set up inmates (and the communities they eventually are released to) for more violence, since inmates are generally kept idle, rendering them dependent on the system and leaving them unprepared to be productive and cooperative enough to avoid resorting to theft and violence in an attempt to meet their needs outside prison. While some say that prisons can serve functions of deterrence and rehabilitation, they actually serve as schools for the study of crime where the most anti-social prisoners teach the rest how to be even more successful in criminal enterprises.

This is not to say that protective detention does not have value. In rare cases (likely involving violence), a suspected individual may be arrested by an SAO and kept in custody for their own safety and that of others (with the possibility of release to an accused individual's chosen SAO, which would be contractually responsible for that individual until the matter is settled). The conditions around actions like this would be standardized between agencies, due to the discipline of constant dealings and their reliance on reciprocal arrangements for such actions. Any organization that could not demonstrate standard justification and consistently humane treatment would be liable for damages and would lose the respect of and working relationships with the industry partners they rely on to function effectively, not to mention the increased risks of violent confrontation.

Those found guilty of a non-violent offense can resolve the situation by paying their fines to restore the victim (or more likely the victim's SAO). Refusal to pay restitution would result in ostracism.

Those found guilty of a violent offense must also pay restitution to the victim (or victim's SAO). However, the nature of their offense will determine whether ostracism alone will be a sufficient consequence for refusal to submit to arbitration and pay restitution. Of course, they would also be the subject of increased contact/observation/tracking/reporting from SAOs in order to manage risk and incentivize compliance.

First-time/low-risk violent offenders would likely be required to pay a fine that includes a recoverable bond to ensure good behavior commensurate with their credible threat level and a standard period of time and/or until satisfactory conditions are reached. Such a bond would be forfeit to the victim if there is any subsequent violence. Refusal to pay would result in ostracism.

Repeat/high-risk violent offenders run the risk of becoming permanently blacklisted and excluded from civilized society, including potential forfeiture of title to property. If circumstances indicate respect for probationary procedures, sincere remorse, and potential for reform, "second chance" opportunities would likely be subject to strict safety/monitoring/liability guidelines and severe financial penalties/bonding requirements.

If an offender is willing but unable to pay, they can bid out their work to potential creditor agencies to pay the fine on their behalf and work off the debt over time. The work conditions would be specified by bidding agencies as part of the contractual arrangement. Such conditions would likely be based on terms acceptable to involved SAOs and risk assessment by the contracting agency, and could range from simple regular payments to supervision to secure facilities. In any case, the more productive an offender is willing and able to be, the faster they can be free of their debt and reclaim their place in society.

It is important to note that private penal firms will have strong incentives to treat detainees well. For starters, a firm with a bad reputation would not receive much business. Mistreating prisoners would make them unable or unwilling to perform anyway, not to mention risks of retaliation and legal action.

Rehabilitation would be far more effective in a private system. Work programs that focus on generating restitution would do more to rehabilitate offenders than any punitive scheme. Private firms would have strong incentives to put the work time of convicts to their most productive use, which would include providing convicts with job training. Job training would make the firm's services more attractive to convicts and SAOs alike, and would make convicts more productive, increasing satisfaction and making early repayment and release more likely. Convicts would have incentives to participate in such training as well, since it would provide them with new and existing marketable skill development that they can put to use for their own benefit, even after release. Society also benefits when convicts are prepared to be productive and independent once released, as an inability to provide for basic needs can be a major factor in theft and other property violations.

Under a private system, convicts have positive incentives for good behavior. The lower the risk to the penal firm, the more likely a convict is to be given more favorable terms of repayment, parole, or other perks in the interest of increasing his productivity.

Private prison alternatives would not function as violent crime schools where resentful abusers live at the expense of their victims, but rather treatment centers where offenders can restore the peace they violated and learn to live satisfying, productive lives.

Severe and Ultimate Ostracism

All systems break down when people refuse to participate in them. Ultimately, those who insist on violent conflict instead of peaceful dispute resolution must be dealt with on those terms. Customary legal systems throughout history have all relied on severe and ultimate ostracism as a threat of last resort for those who commit major offenses and refuse to yield to peaceful dispute resolution. In such cases, the offender is declared an outlaw. Outlawry means the loss of rights to previously recognized property and being subject to being killed without penalty.

Especially heinous offenses like rape and murder cannot be satisfactorily remedied through fines, no matter how large. Those convicted of such severe offenses could possibly be obligated to work for the rest of their life to pay the victim or their family, even though full restitution could never be achieved.

Alternatively, they could be subject to the ultimate ostracism of the death penalty, especially if they are a recalcitrant repeat offender.

The Private Law and Order Hierarchy

In short, obstacles to and disturbances of law and order are best dealt with at the level of personal morality and responsibility. Beyond that, freedom of association allows people to self-select into groups that best promote their values and purposes, as well as incentivize pro-social conduct and internalize costs and benefits of their choices. Risk management tools and processes give individuals and groups practical solutions to avoid and mitigate problems that are not solved by the first two levels. When risk management fails, civilized dispute resolution processes can be used to avoid direct conflict and ensure just and consistent outcomes. At that point, enforcement is based on making things right with victims and maintaining group membership to promote individual reputation preservation/repair and other pro-social outcomes. At this point in the hierarchy, the great majority of conflicts have been avoided or resolved without violent confrontation.

| Morality and Responsibility |
| Freedom of Association |
| Risk Management |
| Dispute Resolution |
| Enforcement |

The last resort of severe or ultimate ostracism would only be indicated under a very rare combination of circumstances: Immoral individuals (level 1) who insist on trespass (level 2) who are able to successfully work around risk management tools and processes (level 3) who refuse to engage in civil dispute resolution (level 4) and/or refuse to abide by the results of that process, against their own self-interest (level 5) who initiate predatory violence against peaceful people (level 5).

Government Interference in Law and Order

As demonstrated above, peace and prosperity have private origins. Paradoxically, the more seamlessly and invisibly effective private governance is, the more people overlook it and misattribute its successes to the state. Likewise, the more the state interferes, the more it co-opts and crowds out private solutions while blaming them for its own failures.

Government agents did not introduce law and order in social and economic affairs. However, many people have been led to believe (by government agents, of course) that without government intervention, markets would lead to chaos and the strong would simply prey upon the weak. This typical viewpoint is overly pessimistic about the ability of individuals and communities to discover and justly enforce the rules that best allow them to peacefully coexist and cooperate, as demonstrated above. More importantly, it is overly optimistic about the state limiting its use of threats and violence. Not only is the general dysfunction of government agencies the world over a famously well-known phenomenon, but the worst atrocities in history have been a result of government predation, not private predation. It is difficult to overstate the harm that results from trusting agents of the state with a monopoly on governance and a moral exemption from aggressive violence.

Arguments in favor of "market augmentation" and the necessity of the "shadow of the state" are based on myths and riddled with various contradictions and fallacies. Perhaps the most popular is the simple false dichotomy of "government provision or no provision" of certain services, especially those related to lawmaking and enforcement.

Not only is state interference in governance and security unnecessary, it causes and suffers from many very serious problems. Government agents operate from within a fundamentally flawed and immoral framework, and they lack the ability, knowledge, incentives, and accountability to provide effective and efficient solutions.

The Descent Into Criminal Law

Over the centuries, the English government slowly expanded its jurisdiction over private security and economic affairs, and Englishmen were systematically forced into compliance by what Richard Laster called "a slowly evolving carrot and stick policy". For example, King Edward III used royal law to create a new crime called "theftbote", which made it illegal for private parties to resolve disputes without submitting to royal courts where the king could get his profits.

Still, protection from and pursuit of criminals was historically handled privately (often by paid specialists), with the goal of justice for victims. Then in the 1750s a magistrate named Henry Fielding began organizing a group of constables and agitating for tax money to be used to pay full salaries. Englishmen opposed the idea on principle, having seen the rise of the police state after the establishment of government police in France in 1667. (French police had always provided the king with detailed information about citizens, opened mail, controlled the press, and arrested and imprisoned innocent people without trial.)

The English people successfully opposed Fielding's government police proposal during his lifetime. Decades later in 1829, Robert Peel was authorized by parliament to form a London metropolitan police department. He faced substantial opposition from the populace (who saw them as government spies), so he tried to pacify them by making the police wear identifiable uniforms.

Between 1829 and 1831, 3000 of the 8000 public police officers hired (nearly 40%) were subsequently fired for unfitness, incompetence, or drunkenness. Despite glaring public failures, the institution of public policing became popular among powerful people who saw that they could shift the cost of protecting their sizable property to taxpayers. These powerful people lobbied against public opinion to support the police, while average citizens still relied on private means for protection and restitution.

The imposition of criminal law meant the abandonment of concern for victims and the incentives that accompany restorative justice. In its place, this new kind of "justice" focused on punishment of offenders at the expense of their victims and innocent neighbors.

For most of Anglo-Saxon history, prisons were largely absent from the justice system. The establishment and expansion of prison as a way of punishing criminals came about only as the government encroached further and further into the court system. Jails ("gaols") were sometimes used by Anglo-Saxons to detain dangerous people awaiting trial, but they were not considered as an appropriate punishment since they forced offenders to be idle, made restitution more difficult, and put additional burdens on the community. But when English kings made private conflict resolution a crime, time to trial was extended to wait for itinerant royal judges. As a result, detention prisons became common. Conditions in such prisons were made awful on purpose with the goal of forcing the accused to plead guilty and pay an amercement (fine). Those who refused could be subject to torture and death if they refused. Prisons soon became profit centers as people were put and kept in prison at their own expense and sold special accommodations if they could afford them. Both jailers and the crown could profit from keeping someone in prison.

Correctional facilities (then known as "houses of correction") were established under Queen Elizabeth, but they were not designed to rehabilitate criminals. The "correction" in question was a matter of forcing the able-bodied poor to work at hard labor. These facilities were also profit centers for the wealthy, who profited from paying below market wages for the labor of innocent prisoners (effectively slaves).

Transportation (deportation of criminals by merchants to be sold into indentured servitude in British colonies) began in 1597, but ran into problems after 1670, as colonies complained about the influx of convicted felons. Wars also interrupted the system, and transporting criminals to the American colonies ended in 1776. English criminals were forced into hard labor in awful conditions, but many of them died and others battled guards and escaped. When the soldiers returned from the American war, crime skyrocketed and there simply were not enough prisons. The British government chose to start transporting prisoners to Australia. By the early 1800s, imprisonment was the major form of punishment for felons, and a series of parliamentary actions in the following decades formalized the tax-funded public prison system.

As government interfered more and more in law and order, torts became crimes, justice became punitive rather than restorative, courts became increasingly biased and monopolized government revenue generators, prisons arose as profit centers, private security personnel became displaced by abusive tax-funded police and surveillance mechanisms, and laws became increasingly overproduced, inconsistent, unenforceable, and counterproductive. None of these intrusions and encroachments were due to any perceived or real market failure.

Government Failure

> It constantly amazes me that defenders of the free market are expected to offer certainty and perfection while government has only to make promises and express good intentions.
> LAWRENCE REED

The following sections provide descriptions and examples of reasons why government interference in law and order is problematic. Some of the reasons and examples apply generally to government and others apply specifically or especially to lawmaking and enforcement functions.

Morality Problems

> I'm going to protect your property and liberty, and I'm going to start by expropriating your property. If you refuse, I'll take what's left of your liberty as well.
> THE STATE

Some of the most fundamental objections to government interference in private life stem from immoral and contradictory assumptions and claims. If compulsion, violence, and monopoly are problems, then how can a coercive monopoly on violence be the solution? If individual rights are paramount, then how can denying and violating them bring about liberty and justice for all? If people cannot be trusted to govern themselves, how can sociopaths who are attracted to positions of power be trusted to govern everyone else? How can forcing people to pay for things they morally object to, do not want, and will not use promote their welfare?

Examples of government morality problems:

- Governments violate private property through various means of extortion ("taxation"), fiat currency manipulation, debt, and eminent domain.
- Governments threaten peaceful people with violence if they refuse to support behavior they consider immoral or counterproductive. For example, if you refuse to pay your taxes for any reason, they steal your property and put you in a cage. If you physically resist the theft and abduction, you will be attacked and killed.
- Governments deny individual self-ownership by threatening and conscripting people to fight and die ("the draft") to promote aggressive authoritarian collectivism. Some governments allow for "conscientious objection" to direct participation in the military, but not for indirect participation through taxation. Clearly, allowing for "conscientious" objections is an economic decision (costs of direct enforceability too high), not a morality decision (no respect for individual conscience).
- Governments also make things funded through taxation indivisible, as if you cannot be willing to pay for things like sewage disposal (although regrettably from a government monopoly) without also being willing to pay for things like unjust war. This is dishonest and manipulative.
- Governments claim to be a benevolent source of alienable rights, but restrict the rights of some individuals in order

to privilege others. Related "might makes right" justifications only demonstrate that discriminatory violence is at the foundation of government.

- Governments selectively force association between individuals and groups, which causes conflict, promotes disorder, and undermines private governance mechanisms that rely on freedom of association. Examples: forced involvement in theft-funded government indoctrination centers ("public schools") and Ponzi schemes ("social security").

- Governments selectively deny association between individuals and groups, which restricts private cooperative relationships and economic growth through voluntary interaction. Examples: border crossing and emigration/immigration restrictions, travel restrictions, trade restrictions, tariffs, and embargoes.

- Governments take credit for the peace and prosperity that result from the internal moral constraints, strong family values, and private governance mechanisms of individuals and voluntary associations while blaming them for its failures.

- Governments are wealth transfer mechanisms that are used by special interests to determine who gains and who loses. Examples: the welfare/warfare state, cronyism, protectionism, occupational licensing, government departments as "jobs projects", etc. In economic terms, government interference is a good on the political market with politically active interest groups on the demand side and legislators and political parties on the supply side. Government naturally expands to restrict competition and extract resources from the public, not to correct so-called market failure.

- Governments justify the abusive behavior of their agents and the negative consequences and externalities of their policies and actions as necessary or unavoidable. (It is interesting to note the similarities between government apologists and those who suffer from pathologies like Stockholm Syndrome/Battered Spouse Syndrome/Post-Traumatic Stress Disorder: justification of abusive behavior, victim blaming, fearful obedience to threats, irrational belief in abusers' omniscience and power, separation anxiety, learned helplessness and passivity, etc.)

Commons Problems

> When the commons problem of public law enforcement services is combined with bureaucratic tendencies to over-produce and inefficiently produce the resulting output, it becomes obvious that the public production of law and order is not an efficient substitute for market production.
> EDWARD STRINGHAM

Government-controlled resources (sometimes referred to euphemistically as "public property") are subject to a number of inherent commons problems. When people's interests conflict and involve the use or disposal of scarce "public" goods, it results in problems of crowding/congestion, permitted use, overuse/overconsumption, underuse/underconsumption, underinvestment, exploitation, free riding, alternative displacement, overprovision/underprovision, and various externalities.

Examples of government commons problems:

- Government monopoly resources are often very overcrowded. The median length of time from filing through trial of civil cases in the US District Court for the Southern District of New York is roughly 33.2 months, and that the median length of time for appeals is 40.8 months. For comparison, the median period of arbitration by the private American Arbitration Association is less than 8 months from start to finish, and the more informal forms of alternative dispute resolution they offer take much less time. When the costs and benefits of such resources are internalized to participants at unit prices, those resources are allocated more wisely and employed more efficiently.
- Government-controlled property invites conflicts over permitted use. Do you have a right to say/express whatever you want? Do you have the right to burn a flag? Do you have the right to march up and down and chant whatever you want? Do you have the right to squat on a road/park/sidewalk? Do you have the right to put up signs? Do you have the right to build religious monuments or statues to controversial figures? Do you have the right for your animals to graze on grassland? The answers depend on whose property is involved.
- Government-controlled property is susceptible to overuse/overconsumption and underuse/underconsumption. Public roads are underproduced, which results in frequent traffic jams. Without private ownership, a lack of incentives to allocate

access to existing roads efficiently also causes both problems of overuse during peak hours and underuse during off-peak hours. Some users take up more space on the roads and cause disproportionate wear and tear with heavy vehicles and loads while others may use them lightly, rarely, or not at all.

- Government-controlled property is susceptible to underinvestment. The American Society of Civil Engineers has given the public infrastructure of the United States an overall grade of D (just above failure). There are too many specifics to cover adequately here, but the US federal government is currently in about 20 trillion dollars of debt and it would take trillions of dollars to repair existing infrastructure in addition to the costs of increasingly necessary new infrastructure. When property rights are assigned to the "public" rather than private parties, people not only overuse the commons, they lack incentives to invest in replacing what they consume.

- Government-controlled property is susceptible to exploitation. When something is everybody's problem, it tends to become nobody's problem. Government agents can easily ignore or subsidize bad behavior on property they control without any personal cost. Littering on government-controlled lands and polluting government-controlled water are clear examples. The effects of such actions are not felt as keenly as by private owners, who are more likely to take greater care to preserve the value and beauty of their resources. Even worse, government agents often grant wealthy corporations exceptions to waste dumping/disposal rules on "public" property (and even private property) in exchange for support, favors, and resources they can personally benefit from.

- Government-provided goods and services are susceptible to freeriding. Millions of people act as free riders on government systems even though the government claims the legal right to demand payment. When providers and recipients are disconnected by disinterested bureaucracies, it is difficult to identify free riders and effectively align their use with proper costs and incentives. Free riders also make loyal supporters of politicians who know how to buy their votes through counterproductive "welfare", make-work jobs projects, progressive taxation, and various other schemes.

- Government provision of goods and services displaces private alternatives. Many government resources are too expensive or difficult for people to access even though they are subsidized by taxation and benefit from eminent domain expropriation. Even when competition is allowed, taxation subsidies crowd out alternative private solutions. Private alternatives like FedEx and UPS have managed to outcompete the US Postal Service despite such a disadvantage, but how many other private alternatives are crowded out by government claiming to act in the "public interest"? Since government often outlaws or undermines private governance and seldom supports it, there is little reason to believe that government interference augments market solutions.

- Government-controlled resources are susceptible to overprovision and underprovision. The overprovision of laws and regulations in the United States has progressed to the point that not even law enforcement personnel are expected to know and understand them. The Code of Federal Regulations alone stands at 150,000 pages and grows every year. Military overproduction is astronomical, thanks in large part to the military industrial complex that ceaselessly lobbies government agents to provoke conflict and waste resources. Underprovision of medical care for veterans by the Department of Veterans Affairs in the United States is absolutely shameful. In 2015, nearly a third of all veterans waiting to be enrolled in the system died before the government even got around to processing their applications. Those who do manage to enroll are subject to systemic neglect and rationing of obsolete or one-size-(doesn't)-fit-all resources.

- Government-controlled property causes various negative externalities and makes internalizing them difficult or impossible. For example, governments exempt themselves from their own pollution regulations and standards, which unsurprisingly has led to the US Government being by far the world's largest polluter (the military alone pollutes more than any other organization in the world). Disinterested and scandal-ridden government agencies not only fail to prevent disasters like the 2010 Deepwater Horizon oil spill (and exempt themselves from any such responsibility), but they are used by companies like BP Oil after the fact to protect powerful interests from liability. Government control of resources severs the natural and necessary connection between rights and responsibilities.

Knowledge Problems

Governments are uniquely ill-suited to provide competent security services or prevent terrorist

attacks for the same reasons they are ill-suited to
provide housing, food, or medical care: they
cannot rationally calculate costs vs. benefits.
Jeff Deist

Solving problems requires knowledge. In addition to
natural limitations on knowledge (especially knowledge of ever-
changing conditions), governments cut themselves off from the
information they need to satisfy those they claim to serve when
they monopolize market functions. How will problems be best
identified? Which of those problems should be addressed, and in
what order? Which potential solutions should be implemented?
How should limited resources be allocated among competing
uses? How should they be sourced, and in what quantity? Are the
final products worth more than they cost to produce? No single
organization of central planners can gather and update all of the
information needed to answer questions like these. Only
decentralized systems that allow for competition and rely on
voluntary participation can provide the input and feedback
necessary to rationally and continually coordinate the behavior of
millions of individuals and satisfy the diverse and changing
demands of customers.

Examples of government knowledge problems:

- Government central planners are subject to the economic
  calculation problem, since bureaucrats cannot rationally
  calculate prices. In voluntary market exchanges, prices
  reflect supply and demand. How much should apples
  cost? If you let people trade for them voluntarily, you can
  answer that question. The same is true of security
  personnel and dispute resolution services. When
  government employees are tempted to make the case that

they are underpaid, they should consider that competition
is not allowed and their salaries are paid with extortion
money.

- Central planners also lack the knowledge to coordinate the
efforts of countless individuals to produce even simple
products, let alone complex ones (see Leonard Read's
short essay "I, Pencil").

- Government monopoly provision relies on speculation
rather than scientific discovery and optimization, since
things that are not allowed to exist cannot be used for
comparison. If government monopolized pizza making
and delivery, it would be impossible to know who makes
the best pizza and who delivers it the fastest. In the
context of law and order, design and enforcement of rules
cannot be optimized (see Rules Without Rulers section
above), and alternatives are unavailable when pretended
solutions are ineffective or make problems even worse.

- Government agents lack the knowledge required to put
resources to their highest and best use. Value is subjective,
and decisions based on value judgments are determined by
marginal utility. Should limited resources be budgeted for
building a new library, road maintenance, enforcement of
non-violent crimes, higher salaries for bureaucrats, or
something else? In a free market, such decisions are
distributed to align with the values of those who bear the
costs. Governments are designed to force one-size-
doesn't-fit-all decisions on all stakeholders.

Incentive Problems

If the consumer is not free to buy security
wherever he pleases, you forthwith see open up a

large profession dedicated to arbitrariness and bad management. Justice becomes slow and costly, the police vexatious, individual liberty is no longer respected, the price of security is abusively inflated and inequitably apportioned, according to the power and influence of this or that class of consumers.
GUSTAVE DE MOLINARI

In voluntary exchange, the incentives of sellers align with the interests of buyers for mutual benefit. Government agencies depend instead on involuntary transfer, which results in incentive problems and invites inefficiency, waste, mismanagement, dysfunction, negligence, moral hazard, counterproductivity, corruption, and abuse.

Examples of government incentive problems:

- Compulsory funding and lack of alternatives weaken incentives to satisfy constituents and use resources wisely. If private companies fail to satisfy customers, customers are free to refuse to give them money and seek alternatives. Government agencies are not subject to such consequences. If government agents ignore, neglect, or mistreat you, you cannot withhold your money or consent without being subject to violence.

- Government is uniquely susceptible to unchecked individual and institutional self-interest. Like others, government agents and institutions have incentives to act in their self-interest. Unlike others, they have access to "public" resources to anonymously promote their own interests at the expense of the often-unsuspecting public. They also claim the right to prohibit competition or crowd it out with subsidies. Unchecked individual self-interest is evident in government workers who idly consume leisure or inefficiently go through the motions at work, even while pursuing overtime opportunities. On the institutional side, government agencies regularly use taxpayer money to lobby for bigger budgets and greater influence, jurisdiction, and discretion.

- Government agencies have incentives to serve and protect special interest groups, not individuals and their natural rights. Government is essentially a wealth transfer mechanism on the supply side of the political market, with special interests on the demand side. Subsidies to favored groups and their accompanying rent-seeking behavior is a testament to this fact. Government policies clearly represent the private interests of politically active pressure groups rather than the "public interest". Among those groups, we find government bureaucrats themselves. For example, the police not only have the opportunity and motivation to selfishly influence legal processes as individuals, but they also collectively function as a very powerful endogenous special interest group that can apply pressure for their own purposes on multiple levels. The "public interest" is commonly among the primary justifications they use to disguise their own conflicts of interest in matters of funding, benefits, monopoly provision, jurisdiction, discretion, legal immunity, militarization, and oversight. Even their elected bosses are incentivized to make policy decisions to their own benefit, which includes securing campaign funding and endorsements from special interest groups.

- Government resource management replaces strong incentives with weak ones. Sensitivity to price and quality is greatly diminished when you are spending someone else's money.

Four Ways to Spend Money		
Your Money	**Others' Money**	
1. High concern for price and quality	2. Low concern for price, high concern for quality	**Spend For Yourself**
3. High concern for price, low concern for quality	4. Low concern for price and quality	**Spend For Others**

Table 1: The private sector spends money in quadrants 1 and 3. Governments spend money in quadrants 2 and 4.

- Government externalizes consequences and participates in moral hazard. When you are immune from the consequences of your decisions, you lack incentive to minimize their impact. With this in mind, it shouldn't come as a surprise that government actions are often overly aggressive and costly. When government agents make bad decisions, taxpayers are on the hook to bail them out. For example, government agents have nothing to lose and everything to gain by filing frivolous, discriminatory, or vindictive lawsuits through their respective agencies. Taxpayers are forced to pick up the tab, win or lose.
- Government often ignores or exacerbates problems because of perverse incentives. Public police have no economic incentives to prevent offenses or restore property to victims. They are primarily concerned with

making arrests and imprisoning criminals. (Arrest statistics are convenient, since they are easy to measure and can be publicized as justification for various encroachments.) Prosecutors have similar issues with conviction statistics. Clearly, government systems are designed to process criminals, not to prevent crimes or make victims whole. They incentivize addressing problems ex post rather than ex ante and focus on symptoms rather than causes. In these government processes, victims (especially poor and disenfranchised ones) are often reduced to tools and pieces of evidence. Some incentives are so perverse that they actually promote organized crime (e.g. vice prohibition schemes) and create victims (e.g. arrest quotas, see also "rat effect"). Even with the best of individual intentions, how legislators, bureaucrats, police, and jurists act depends heavily on their institutional incentives.

- Government is prone to corruption and abuse of authority. Much of political corruption is a natural consequence of the discretionary authority of government officials. This is especially the case with victimless crimes like prostitution, gambling, and narcotics, as they are particularly lucrative and easy to overlook (even more so in a climate of increasing overcriminalization and unenforceability). Government agents also have a lot of official favors they can sell. They can directly or indirectly fund massive operations. They can grant monopoly privileges and exclusive government contracts. In many places, bribes and kickbacks have essentially become standard operating procedure with government officials. It has been said that power tends to corrupt. Coercive power and discretionary authority are particularly dangerous in this regard.

Ability Problems

> Depending on the severity of its deficiencies, government may be anything from an inept protector of property rights and facilitator of economic exchange, to their primary disruptor.
> EDWARD STRINGHAM

Some problems are unavoidable and must simply be lived with. Other problems are manufactured or greatly overstated by governments to instill fear and promote their agenda. But even when problems are real and solvable, government solutions are often absent, irrelevant, unfeasible, unaffordable, unsustainable, ineffective, unenforceable, inefficient, poorly implemented, and even counterproductive.

Examples of government ability problems:

- Government is simply unfit to provide solutions to sophisticated problems. Government authority relies on coercion, and as the old adage states: if the only tool you have is a hammer, everything looks like a nail that needs pounding. Without persuasion and competitive advantage in an environment of free association, authoritarian violence initiates and escalates conflict rather than avoiding and resolving it. The clumsy and heavy hand of government is a tool for control and destruction, not peaceful cooperation and prosperity. In the words of William Grigg: "Government has one tool, and that's violence. It has one method of operation, and that's aggression. It has one strategy, and that's escalation."

- Government largely relies on private groups to write laws and regulations and grants them special privileges as de facto regulators. Conveniently, any failures can be blamed on market forces and used as justification for more government interference while successes can be misattributed to government interference and used as further justification for more of the same. Either way, such privileges are used to benefit special interests (both private and governmental) at the expense of everyone else.

- Government offers irrelevant solutions to many problems. The problems in question are often manufactured as a justification for bundles of ready-made control mechanisms that are intentionally named to conceal details, mask intentions, and marginalize critics (see: The Patriot Act and the establishment of the TSA). Like they say, they never let a good crisis go to waste.

- Government solutions are often unfeasible, unaffordable, and unsustainable. Even well-meaning central planners are subject to economic realities in their pursuits of utopian fantasy. Denying and defying scarcity and resource limitations has led to widespread bankrupt Ponzi schemes (like Social Security and other government pension and benefit programs) that rely not only on increased costs to new participants, but also on increasingly unpayable transgenerational debt. Promises may be the one thing government agents can make in seemingly unlimited quantities.

- Many government solutions are unenforceable. Government laws and regulations are generally overproduced. They can also contradict each other, especially when jurisdictions overlap. On the enforcement side, there are observability limitations, resource limitations, and conflicting priorities, none of which are required to be addressed by the enacting legislators. In addition to related moral objections, laws against victimless crimes are particularly problematic in this regard.

- Government solutions are relatively ineffective. For example, according to the Bureau of Justice Statistics, only about half of violent crimes and about a third of property crimes in the US each year are even reported to police, and most of the crimes that are reported to police are not solved. The odds that government police will successfully apprehend the suspect of a violent crime is approximately 22%. The odds for property crime are even more dismal at approximately 6%. Numbers like these are especially frustrating given the lack of incentives for government agents to prevent such offenses in the first place. Furthermore, even when police do identify a suspect, the focus of their efforts is on punishing them rather than providing restitution for victims.

- Government solutions are inefficient. In addition to incentive problems resulting from monopoly privileges, government services are not designed to specialize, innovate, restructure, or otherwise adapt to market conditions. Government solutions are also frequently overlapping and duplicative, with multiple agencies at multiple levels claiming to do the same job. Responsibility for execution of potentially effective solutions is also often fragmented between agencies, resulting in partial or poor implementation. Even government solutions that more or less serve their intended purposes are provided at high cost and after long delays.

- Government makes some problems significantly worse by wasting resources on meddling with them. Counterproductive boondoggles like alcohol prohibition and the drug war cost many times more money and lives than they could ever save.

Accountability Problems

> In business, failure is met with losses or liquidation; in government, failure is met with larger budgets.
> CHASE RACHELS

If private organizations fail to satisfy customers and play by the rules, they go out of business. If they offer poor service at high prices, customers can refuse to buy. If they are fraudulent, abusive, or in breach of contract, customers can hold them liable. Government is under no such constraints. It demands funding by threat of violence. It makes the rules and exempts itself from them. It answers to no external authority. It allows for no competition, but claims the privileged position of being absolutely necessary. Short of defiance, there are no practical ways to effectively hold government accountable.

Examples of government accountability problems:

- There can't be consent of the governed when government is "an offer you can't refuse". Government operations are funded by extortion (euphemistically referred to as "taxation"). Without the ability to withhold money and consent, how can government agents be expected or required to justify or change their behavior? For example, if the police had to satisfy those they claim to serve in order to earn their business, they would act more thoughtfully, humbly, and respectfully. As it stands, they are guaranteed payment by taxation whether they do a terrible job or not. Even when governments are clearly corrupt, negligent, and abusive, their critics are held in contempt for suggesting alternatives to the centralized coercive government model itself.

- Government agents are considered above the law. It should come as no surprise that a group with a monopoly on making and enforcing laws would exempt themselves from those laws. "Qualified immunity" was established by the US Supreme court in a case known as Harlow v. Fitzgerald. It means that "public servants" (including police officers, of course) cannot be held civilly liable for violating a person's rights unless the officer violates a law that they could reasonably be expected to know and unless the victim's rights are established "beyond dispute". That's right, law enforcement is not "reasonably" expected to know all of the laws they enforce and cannot be held accountable to victims for violating them (in contrast to those they "serve", who are told that ignorance of the law is no excuse). How well should police officers know and understand the laws they are sworn to uphold? The Supreme Court answered this in an 8-1 decision in Heien v. North Carolina by saying that police don't actually need to know the law and that they can enforce the laws incorrectly if their mistakes are determined to be "reasonable" by fellow government agents. What limits are there to police authority if they can claim ignorance of

the law and are then immune from the consequences of
their actions?

- Government is subject to no external authority. As the old
  Latin saying goes: Quis custodiet ipsos custodies? Who
  watches the watchers? In a free society, individuals and
  firms must bear the costs of their own behavior (no "just
  doing my job" excuses allowed) and are kept in check by
  market forces of competition and endogenous regulation
  by peers and trusted industry auditors. Government
  agents can secretly break the law and have their crimes
  and abuses protected as "classified". If necessary, they can
  investigate their own wrongdoing behind closed doors.
  The government also claims the authority to arbitrate
  conflicts involving its own agents or agencies. The idea
  that government can effectively check and balance itself is
  a fantasy.

Summary

Here is a summarized comparison of the features of private and government systems for law and order. Which system do you prefer?

Private Law and Order	Government Interference in Law and Order
Consistent with natural law and property rights	Violates natural law and property rights
Justice as protection and restitution	Justice as revenge and punishment
Freedom of association / disassociation	Forced integration / segregation
Promotes responsibility and strong families	Distorts responsibility and family relationships
Based on consent and reciprocity	Based on coercion and authoritarian violence
Based on the precautionary assumptions that men are fallible and that power corrupts	Assumes that those in positions of power will be of superior intellectual ability and moral character
Ongoing flexible discovery of optimal rules	Rigid overproduction of sub-optimal rules
Bias for root cause analysis and peaceful prevention	Bias for fixation on symptoms and violent escalation

Private Law and Order	Government Interference in Law and Order
Bias for swift economical dispute resolution	Bias for self-serving bureaucratic formalities
Sophisticated customized solutions	Clumsy one-size-fits-all-or-none model
Offenders support themselves	Offenders live at the expense of victims
Offenders can learn and grow and become more self-reliant	Offenders forced to be idle and unproductive and rely on the system
Offenders offered redemption	Offenders offered more criminal association
Funded by voluntary exchange	Funded by extortion
Serve and protect individuals and their rights	Serve and protect special interests
Wealth protection mechanisms	Wealth transfer mechanisms
Responsibility and respect for private property	Conflicts over and exploitation of "public property"
Tendency for equilibrium of production and use	Tendency for imbalance of production and use
Tendency for sustainable investment	Tendency for underinvestment and unfunded liabilities
Internalization of costs and	Stubborn externalities and

Private Law and Order	Government Interference in Law and Order
benefits	freeriding
Market pricing	Economic calculation problem
Division of labor and spontaneous order	Monolithic inefficiency
Scientific discovery and verification	Speculation and untestable claims
Constituents are persuaded and satisfied	Constituents are bullied and resented
Strong incentives to innovate	Strong incentives to maintain status quo
Strong incentives for low price and high quality	Weak incentives for low price and high quality
Tendency to use resources wisely	Tendency to waste resources
Tendency for aligned incentives	Tendency for perverse incentives
No special privileges to abuse or stolen resources to sell	Invites corruption and abuse of authority
Reliance on reputation and earned trust	Reliance on positional authority
Failures result in losses and liquidation	Failures result in larger budgets

Private Law and Order	Government Interference in Law and Order
Transparency and equality before the law	Secrecy, self-monitoring, and qualified immunity
Competition and endogenous market regulation	Monopoly and lack of exogenous oversight
Model is decentralized, making it fault-tolerant and resilient and allowing for graceful responses to localized failures	Model is centralized, making it vulnerable to hostile takeover, catastrophic failure, and total systemic collapse

The Minarchist Dilemma

> The fatal error of classical liberals lies in their failure to realize that their ideal is theoretically impossible, as it contains the seed of its own destruction, precisely to the extent that it includes the necessary existence of a state (even a minimal one), understood as the sole agent of institutional coercion.
>
> JESUS HUERTA DE SOTO

Some say that coercive government is a "necessary evil". However, that is just another way of saying "I am blind to the private voluntary solutions that surround me, I choose to deny and justify the immoral and abusive behavior of those who call themselves 'government', and I cannot imagine how my fearful demands could be satisfied by anything other than stealing resources and bullying people." Trading the possibility of private predation for the guarantee of public predation is a fool's bargain, and justifying it is a self-defense mechanism of the naïve.

Minarchists are generally comfortable with the idea of reducing the size and power of government, but are uncomfortable following through on their reasoning to its logical conclusions. If private solutions are better at providing food and clothing, they are better at providing law and order for the same reasons. On the other hand, if government were better at providing law and order, it would be better at providing food and clothing, too.

All government apologists consider themselves minarchists; they just differ somewhat in their definitions of what is minimal. Even socialists just claim to provide minimal necessary services. Minarchism is just the early stages of socialism. Saying that a small amount of socialism is beneficial is like saying a small amount of cancer is beneficial. Why not eliminate it completely?

Some say that rule by violence is unavoidable, and that the only way to protect people from violent gangs is to empower an official violent gang and ask that it limit itself to being nice. The false choice between being subject to unmitigated chaos and supporting organized crime lies at the heart of this utopian fantasy. Is society safer from power grabs when it is run by armed authoritarians with a monopoly on violence?

Government has never been effectively limited. Every aspect of government interference in law and order was initially very limited. As lust for power, bureaucratic sprawl, and rent seeking take hold, "limited" government inevitably grows into a tyrant.

The American secessionists who signed the anarchistic declaration of independence clearly wanted to be free to organize their lives as they saw fit. In their obvious attempts to limit government tyranny, they designed what they saw as a limited government. Unfortunately, that state is only "limited" to monopoly control of legislation, military, police, courts, the monetary system, essential infrastructure, and education. It is funded by extortion, and claims jurisdiction over all matters of commerce and general welfare. In other words, it has all the tools necessary to establish and maintain absolute tyranny. It is no wonder that current political debates center around whether or not the government should limit its jurisdiction and influence at all.

> But whether the Constitution really be one thing, or another, this much is certain – that it has either authorized such a government as we have had, or has been powerless to prevent it. In either case, it is unfit to exist.
> LYSANDER SPOONER

Conclusion

Governments do a lot of bad things. They also try to do some good things, but they do them badly.

It should be clear at this point that the burden of proof is on those who claim that government interference in law and order is necessary and preferable, given not only its dismal track record, but also the fact that it lacks the knowledge, ability, incentive, and accountability to improve on private governance. The government legal system simply co-opted and perverted a superior legal system, interrupting its continued evolution.

Private voluntary solutions are not perfect, but they provide more order, choice, liberty, peace, and justice. They promote wealth creation and civilizational development. They are relatively free of violence. They are less expensive, and more efficient, safe, flexible, resilient, consistent, innovative, sustainable, and sophisticated. They work in small and simple contexts with homogenous groups and repeatable interactions. They work in large and complex contexts within heterogeneous groups and non-repeat interactions across political boundaries, long distances, and extended time periods.

I recognize that there is significant and seemingly overwhelming opposition to a free society. I don't expect it to be fully established in my lifetime, but the further along the societal spectrum we can move toward liberty, the better. There are also reasons to be optimistic about moving toward that ideal. In recent years, confidence in government institutions has dropped dramatically, and participation in private solutions is on the rise in many areas. People have grown increasingly accustomed to the benefits of decentralized systems like the internet, even if they fail to recognize it. New technologies like distributed manufacturing and blockchain ledgers can make government interference more difficult. The fundamental tasks for those who seek a free society today are in education and innovation.

Author's Note

I hope for a peaceful and decentralized future where freedom of association allows for people to participate in the kinds of groups and governance they prefer rather than having it forced on them by others. I don't know how many people are ready for that, but it's always a good time to move in the right direction. In the meantime, we can remind ourselves and each other about the many private sources of social order that surround us every day.

Perhaps there will be a sizeable independent-minded minority of peaceful and productive people who have the ability and the willingness to defend themselves against authoritarian central planners. I would love to see my descendants thriving in such a society, and I think maybe you would, too. Whether we live to see it or not, let's make sure the tree of liberty gets as much water and light as we can give it.

A Note of Thanks and Invitation

Thank you for taking the time to read this book. I hope it has helped you see that government interference does not make people more safe than they would be in a private law society.

I would love to hear your feedback. If reading this book sparked thoughts, questions, or even respectful disagreement, I'd be very grateful if you'd share a quick review on Amazon or Goodreads or wherever you found it. If you can share an image or video of your favorite parts, that's even more helpful. You can leave a review by visiting https://www.amazon.com/dp/B0GYQPYFBZ or by scanning this QR code:

Please also feel free to reach out to me with your thoughts using the contact form at: https://www.livingvoluntary.com/about-me/.

If you would like to read more or sign up for my mailing list, you can do so at https://www.livingvoluntary.com/voluntas-press/.